If You Don't Vote, You Don't Count

Vernon Dahmer's Fight for Equality

By Rochelle "Shelly" Dahmer

Illustrated by Jackson Muthoni

I dedicate this book to Mrs. Ellie Jewel Dahmer and the Dahmer Family in their quest for justice for Mr. Vernon Dahmer Sr. Also, I thank my husband, Phillip, and my children who always believed in me.

—R.D.

If You Don't Vote, You Don't Count

Vernon Dahmer's Fight for Equality

By Rochelle "Shelly" Dahmer

Lungs filling with smoke, he could hardly catch his breath. Bullets whizzed by. All he could think about was the safety of his family.

He shouted to his wife to take the children out the back window and run to the woods. Relentlessly, the shooters fired shot after shot.

Sadly, Vernon had known that this day would come.

As a growing southern boy, Vernon Ferdinand Dahmer Sr. loved his life in the piney woods of south Mississippi.

He enjoyed spending the warm summer afternoons fishing and catching bream in the fresh, clear creeks that ran through the family land.

He worked alongside his father and brothers, cutting and hauling the timber that was cradled in the deep dark pockets of nature.

While the dew still glistened on the blades of grass, he trudged to the weathered barn to milk the cows and feed the clucking chickens.

He relished the fresh grass scent that carried through the barn from the newly cut bales of hay.

Basket in hand, he plucked warm eggs from the hens' nests for that day's breakfast.

He helped plant collard greens, yellow ears of sweet corn, and watermelons that grew to gigantic sizes. His family planted peanut plants that grew green and regal.

As Vernon grew into a strong young man and his father grew weary with age, he took over the everyday operations of the farm.

His responsibility increased as his siblings left Mississippi. They sought a loosening of the grips of the oppressive Jim Crow laws and restrictions of the South. Restaurants, movie theatres, and other public places were segregated, which meant blacks and whites were separate.

Worse, black citizens were beaten or lynched for minor offenses.

The only son to stay on the farm, Vernon became a successful businessman.

He would go on to woo his future wife, a teacher named Ellie Jewel Davis with treasures from the land. Smitten by his actions and kindness, Ellie loved Vernon.

Together, they created a strong union of marriage and support while living a comfortable life with seven sons and one daughter.

With a large family to provide for, Vernon continued the family tradition with King Cotton and timber.

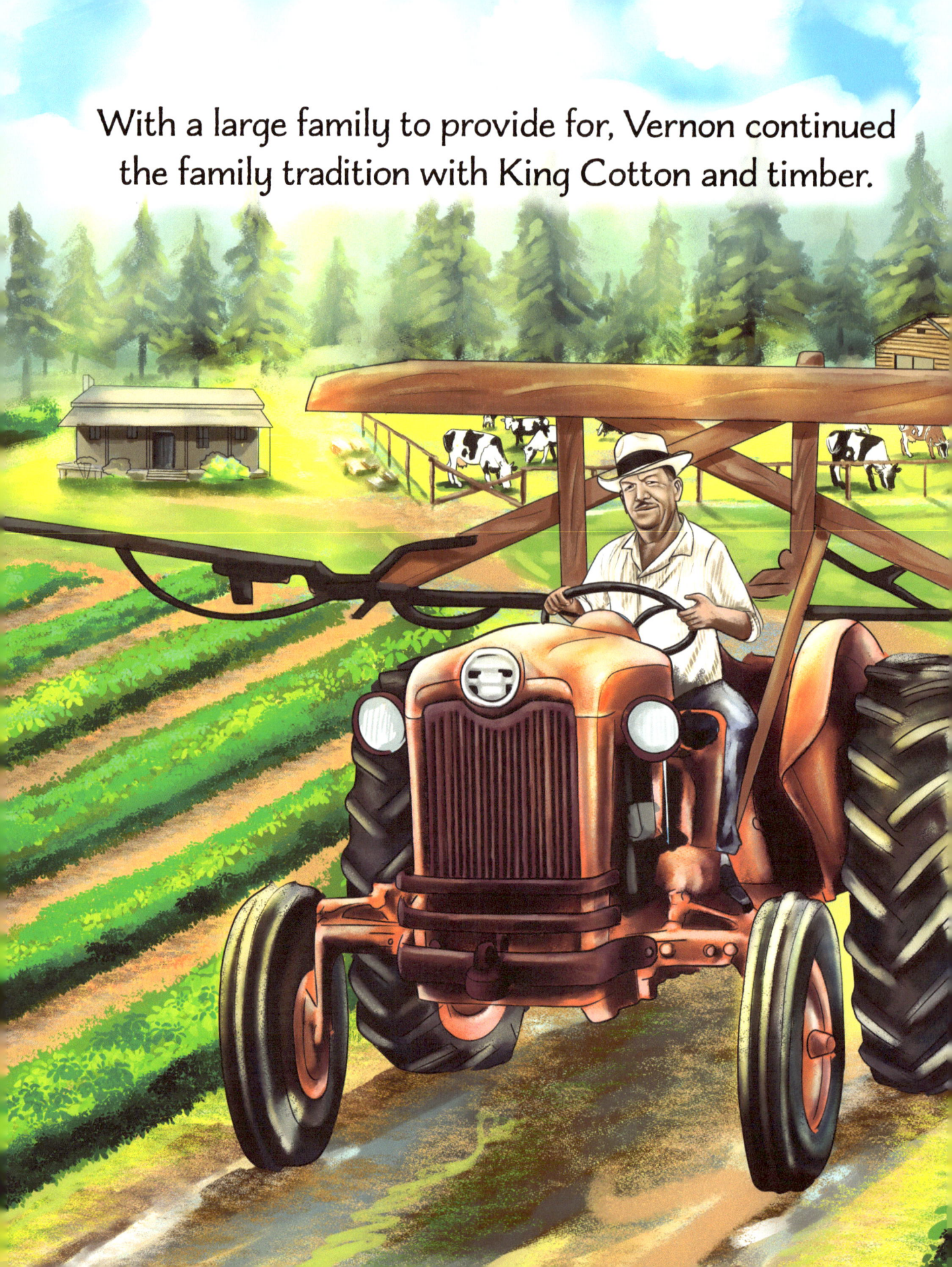

He started a sawmill and lumber business. Also, he opened a grocery store that gave blacks a place to shop and let many buy on credit.

As he rose to new heights in his farming and business life, he brought his community and others with him.

One summer, out-of-state college students called Freedom Riders banded together to help organize voting registration drives in Mississippi.

However, during Freedom Summer, the young activists were met with violence and resistance from some locals. The students endured harassment, beatings, and even death.

To buffer the hate, Vernon and Ellie welcomed the student activists to their home for a picnic.

After lunch, Vernon taught them the intricate parts of the soft, fluffy balls of cotton. Ellie remembers this day vividly.

When asked to describe Vernon, Ellie said "he was a Christian." He sang in the church choir. He taught the Bible in Sunday School with fervor and passion.

This passion was also found in the Civil Rights Movement. After years of restrictions due to race, Vernon could no longer bear the thought of his community working and tolling but never receiving the rights of citizenship and voting.

The laws of the day, plus harassment and threats of violence held many African Americans silent with no political voice.

Consequently, his ongoing desire for equal rights came at a critical time. Many saw this moment as a crucial opportunity to combat segregation and secure voting rights.

So, Vernon joined the NAACP (National Association for the Advancement of Colored People), an organization devoted to improving life for African Americans.

Thus, Vernon came to the attention of the Ku Klux Klan with his civil rights activism, and this push to encourage more blacks to register to vote.

Typically called the KKK, this vigilante group believed blacks were inferior, had to be kept in their place, and had no right to a political voice.

Fueled by hatred, the Klan intimidation tactics kept the family on alert. To ensure constant protection from danger, they slept in shifts.

Vernon received threatening phone calls, harassment, and damage to his property with windows shot out and a barn fire.

His insurance was canceled on his home and business. His longtime relationship with local banks was severed.

However, this turn of events did not deter Vernon. He continued to try and register to vote but was turned away each time, rejected due to a literacy test that was designed to discourage black citizens from trying to vote.

Even after the rejection, he was determined to press on toward his goal of first-class citizenship and voting rights for disenfranchised blacks. Vernon often said, "A man needed to do his own thinking."

As a way to increase citizen participation, he provided transportation to the courthouse for those attempting voter registration, but then he decided to take it to another level.

The passing of the Voting Rights Act of 1965 legally forbade officials from threatening or tricking blacks into not voting. Even with federal intervention, some states still required a two-dollar poll tax for state elections in 1966, along with literacy tests.

However, more African Americans attempted to register to vote but were met with retaliation from some locals.

Therefore, the Tax Collector allowed Vernon to keep a voter registration book at the Dahmer Grocery Store and accept the poll tax.

The new plan was publicized on the local radio station. This new development angered Klan members who were already plotting to silence Vernon with death.

Many brave white and black activists had already been killed or brutally attacked by the Klan and other segregationists.

The family understood Vernon's actions angered those who wanted racial division, but due to the recent federal laws, they never imagined his life was in jeopardy.

In the past to prepare for violence, the Dahmers lived with extreme caution. However, on the evening of January 9, 1966, they settled into a comfortable slumber.

Under the veil of darkness in the early morning hours of January 10, 1966, the Dahmer home and grocery store were the target of a firebomb attack by a group of KKK night riders while the family slept.

Roused from sleep by an outside noise, Ellie woke Vernon, leading him to protect his family.

On that tragic night, Vernon's family escaped their burning home as he bravely fought back against the attackers, but he died from his injuries.

Some of Vernon's last words were "In this society, if you don't vote, you don't count." Even on his deathbed, he never wavered in his beliefs or love for his family.

Sadly, with federal laws in place that gave blacks voting rights, Vernon received his voter registration card after his funeral.

Dahmer's bravery welled up in a tumultuous and frightening time to empower and influence others around him. Because he dared to dream, Vernon Dahmer died on that fateful day, but his sacrifice and the sacrifice of others have moved America forward and given blacks a voice and a place in the country.

Politician

Astronaut

Mrs. Ellie Jewel

Spokesperson

Dr. Donavon Dahme

Though social and political issues are far from perfect, the country has made tremendous strides. Now, there are black astronauts. Now, there are black millionaires and billionaires. Now, there are blacks in major roles in movies and television. Now, there are more black doctors than ever before.

And because of the efforts of Vernon and others like him, only recently the United States of America had its first black President who served two brilliant terms, representing all Americans, of all creeds and colors, Barack Obama.

Fifty years later, there are still injustices, but the lives given for freedom were not given in vain. So, America can continue to be a beacon of light for many seeking the opportunity of a better life.

Author's Notes

Vernon Ferdinand Dahmer, Sr. was born on March 10, 1908, in the Kelly Settlement in Forrest County, Mississippi.

Living in the early 1900s, a young Vernon developed a heart for his community as he observed the lack and poverty all around him. On the heels of post-slavery and war, along with The Great Depression, he would witness his community of Kelly Settlement lay stagnant as the city of Hattiesburg was slowly prospering for others but not for African Americans.

He endured the grips of discrimination and hate, but a longing began to simmer in his soul. Vernon wanted more in his life.

Raised by a white father and a multiracial mother, his family received benefits that others did not possess; however, he longed for citizenship and recognition for all. He believed that if a person was paying taxes and striving to be a good citizen, they deserved the rewards of first-class citizenship.

Sadly, he watched as African Americans were treated as second-class citizens with low-paying jobs, along with substandard housing and schools, because many of the city leaders held on to their Confederate ideology.

However, this fact did not deter him from longing for equality for himself and other African Americans. Because of his deep beliefs in equality for all, his focus would drive him to work hard and push for the rights that he knew that everyone deserved.

He would motivate many people with his mantra that stated–if you don't vote, you don't count. Vernon F. Dahmer's mantra of "if you don't vote, you don't count" resonates in our country today, but Vernon Dahmer spoke these words in the early 20th century.

His quest to be a first-class citizen turned his world upside down, but his bravery, recognized by presidents, continues to motivate others to achieve goals against all odds.

Mr. Dahmer died on January 10, 1966, at 57 years old.

Honoring Vernon Dahmer: A Legacy of Courage and Equality

Since Vernon Dahmer's tragic death in 1966, he has received significant recognition nationally, at the state level, and locally for his contributions to the Civil Rights Movement.

- **Hattiesburg, Mississippi, honored him by naming a street and park after him.** They also established a memorial to Dahmer in the park in 1986. In 2020, they dedicated a statue to commemorate Vernon Dahmer Sr.'s work as a civil rights leader. Officially unveiled at the Forrest County Courthouse, the statue honors Dahmer's brave struggle for voting rights and equality.

- **Mississippi State Recognition:** In 2016, Mississippi lawmakers honored Vernon Dahmer on the 50th anniversary of his death. His widow, Ellie Dahmer, and several relatives received a plaque in his honor.

- **Mississippi Civil Rights Museum:** This exhibit highlights his significant contributions to the Civil Rights Movement, particularly his efforts to secure voting rights for African Americans. The museum showcases his courageous fight against racial injustice and honors his legacy as a civil rights leader.

- **National Civil Rights Museum:** The National Civil Rights Museum in Washington, D.C., has recognized Vernon Dahmer for his contributions to the fight for voting rights and equality.

- **Museum of the Courageous:** The Museum of the Courageous, located in San Francisco, features stories of individuals who have shown courage in the face of hate-honored Dahmer.

- **Federal Recognition:** In 1998, a jury found the former Ku Klux Klan leader guilty of murder and arson related to Dahmer's death, underscoring the federal government's dedication to achieving justice for civil rights activists.

These awards highlight the continuing importance of Vernon Dahmer's work in the struggle for civil rights and equal voting. His bravery and dedication continue to inspire future generations, and his legacy continues.

References

Bates, Ruth. Before There Was a Mississippi. Nebraska: Morris   Publishing.   1999. Print.

Dahmer, Dennis. Interview. Conducted by Rochelle Dahmer, 19 May 2023.

Dahmer, Vernon. Interview. Conducted by Rochelle Dahmer, 22 Aug. 2015.

Dahmer, Ellie. Dahmer, Bettie. "They Intended to Get All of Us January The 10th, 1966." https://www.npr.org/series/4516989/storycorps.

Erb, Phillips Kelly. "For Election Day, A History of The Poll Tax in America." 5 November 2018. www.forbes.com.

"Freedom Summer." Wikipedia, Wikimedia Foundation, 1 Mar. 2017, en.wikipedia.org/wiki/Freedom_Summer. Accessed 2 Aug. 2023.

Hattiesburg American, March 12, 1968

Hattiesburg American, February 13, 1994

Leonard, Caroline. "UM Votes: Exploring the History of Voting Suppression in MS." The University of Mississippi: Diversity and Community. www.dce.olemiss.edu

"Library of Congress-Civil Rights History Project: Ellie Dahmer." YouTube, uploaded by Library of Congress, 30 Nov. 2015, www.youtube.com@loc.

"Library of Congress-Civil Rights History Project: Vernon Dahmer." YouTube, uploaded by Library of Congress, 1 Dec. 2015, www.youtube.com@ loc.Merriam-Webster.com Dictionary,

Merriam-Webster, https://www.merriam-webster.com/ dictionary/inheritance. Accessed 6 Jun. 2023.

"American Democracy: A Great Leap of Faith." National Museum of American History, americanhistory. si.edu/democracy-exhibition/vote-voice/keeping-vote/state-rules-federal-rules/literacy-tests.

Morris, Benjamin. Hattiesburg, Mississippi: A History of the Hub City. Charleston, N.C.: The History Press. 2014. Print

Renegadesouth, et al. "The Family Origins of Vernon Dahmer, Civil Rights Activist." Renegade South, 9 Oct. 2018, renegadesouth.wordpress.com/2009/12/06/the-family-origins-of-vernon-dahmer-civil-rights-activist/.

Author Rochelle Dahmer, a retired educator and wife of Vernon Dahmer's grandson, has always loved writing. This is her third self-published book.

Rochelle lives in Hattiesburg, Miss., with her husband, Phillip. She is the mother to two, the stepmom to three, and also the step-nana to six grand-children and three daughters-in-law.

Illustrator Jackson Muthoni is a Kenyan artist.

In the turbulent era of the 1950s and 60s, amidst the battle for civil rights and racial equality, a brave figure named Vernon Dahmer emerged. His goal was first-class citizenship! This man did not allow society's ideals to keep him from his dreams. He overcame numerous obstacles that kept most men mired in poverty. He would lose his life before his dreams were recognized, but his influence and impact are still felt in our society today.

"If you don't vote, you don't count."
–Vernon Ferdinand Dahmer Sr.

Other Books by Rochelle "Shelly" Dahmer

Nonfiction Books

Writing Made Easy: A Step-by-Step Guide
(If Writing is NOT Your "THING")

How to Self-Publish Your Dream Book Over 50: A Step-by-Step Guide to Finally Be a Published Author

Fiction Picture Books

"Nightmares in the Little Poster Bed"

Connect with Rochelle "Shelly" Dahmer

shellydahmer@gmail.com

www.writershellydahmer.com

facebook.com/rdahmer

instagram.com/shellyscreativelife

www.youtube.com/ShellysCreativeLife

Vocabulary Words List

1. civil rights activist
2. Civil Rights Movement
3. disenfranchised
4. equality
5. empower
6. equality
7. Freedom Summer
8. Jim Crow Laws
9. Ku Klux Klan
10. NAACP
11. poll tax
12. segregation
13. tumultuous
14. voting
15. voting rights
16. Voting Rights Act

Vocabulary and Definitions

Civil Rights Activist: An individual who actively campaigns for the civil rights of all people.

Civil Rights Movement: A social movement in the United States during the 1950s and 1960s, aiming to end racial discrimination and secure equal rights under the law for African Americans.

Disenfranchised: Deprived of the right to vote or other rights.

Empower: To give someone the authority or power to do something, especially in the context of marginalized groups gaining power and control over their lives.

Equality: The state of being equal, especially in status, rights, and opportunities.

Freedom Summer: A 1964 voter registration drive aimed at increasing the number of registered Black voters in Mississippi.

Jim Crow Laws: State and local laws that enforced racial segregation in the Southern United States from the late 19th century until the 1960s.

Ku Klux Klan: A white supremacist hate group that has historically targeted African Americans and other minorities.

NAACP (National Association for the Advancement of Colored People): A civil rights organization founded in 1909 to fight for the rights of African Americans.

Poll Tax: A tax levied as a prerequisite for voting, often used to disenfranchise African American voters.

Segregation: The enforced separation of different racial groups in a country, community, or establishment.

Tumultuous: Characterized by disorderly commotion or disturbance.

Voting: The act of making a choice among alternatives in an election.

Voting Rights: The legal rights protecting individuals' ability to participate in the electoral process.

Voting Rights Act: A landmark federal law passed in 1965 that prohibits racial discrimination in voting.

www.ingramcontent.com/pod-product-compliance
Lightning Source LLC
Chambersburg PA
CBHW041553120626
46551CB00002B/191